Gidget, I'm Coming, I'm Coming HOME

Jake Brown

ISBN 979-8-88644-290-8 (Paperback)
ISBN 979-8-88644-291-5 (Digital)

Covenant Books
11661 Hwy 707
Murrells Inlet, SC 29576
www.covenantbooks.com

INTRODUCTION

This is basically a true story about two dogs and events in their lives that changed their relationship forever. They belonged to a family, but in truth, they belonged only to each other.

Queenie was the oldest of seven miniature dachshund puppies, and Gidget was the youngest. All of the dogs in between had been sold, but no one seemed to want these two dogs until we came to look at them. We were told that the two had been together since birth and that if one was to go, the other one had to accompany.

We lived in a small mountain town in rural Colorado and the two dogs made themselves at home immediately. Queenie was dominative, and Gidget was very subservient and intimidated.

The story really begins when Queenie's one and only puppy comes for a visit over the Memorial Day weekend.

I

The morning sun revealed a crisp, cloudless blue sky forecasting good weather for the Memorial Day weekend. The air was chilly, but inside the doghouse, it was warm and cozy. Queenie and Gidget lay in the corner atop the thick, soft green shag carpeting, which lay over the floor and halfway up the walls. As was customary, Queenie lay in the corner next to the wall, and Gidget lay close keeping Queenie's exposed side warm.

The dogs were sleeping soundly and failed to hear the pickup pull into the driveway and stop, the doors open, and the passengers exit making their way to the backdoor of the house. In the arms of Boy was a dark brown bundle squirming to be placed on the ground. One short bark from the bundle immediately alerted Queenie whose rotund body moved quickly, jumping to her feet, leaving Gidget's frail little body thrashing in the air to right herself and figure out just what had happened.

Queenie ran from the doghouse, knowing instinctively that the Man had brought his son to visit over the Memorial Day weekend, and with the son had come Puppy, Queenie's one and only puppy, the light of her life, her delight, the one she loved enormously. She was giddy with excitement. Queenie was instantly licking the little dog, nuzzling, circling, whining with joy that Puppy had come for a visit. Looking the little dog over, she knew that he had grown, his color and coat slick and shiny, his tail curved and upright just as a show dog would hold its tail, his paws large and thick. He was a "beautiful dachshund." She was overly thrilled to see her one and only after seven months, and my, how he had changed.

Gidget trotted to the back door to observe and try to find out what was happening. No sooner had she made her appearance, wagging her tail in delight to see Puppy, then Queenie immediately curled her lip, jaw set, giving Gidget that low, guttural growl letting her know that she was not welcome and being put in her place and was to make an immediate retreat. Gidget walked slowly back to the doghouse and lay down feeling totally rejected, half inside the house and half out with her head on her paws as she always did. Queenie was *the queen* and never failed to let Gidget be aware of that fact.

Queenie's head was filling with the travels and the reacquaintances she and Puppy would have with the time that he was visiting.

First, she would take Puppy to see Sally and her little girls, then they would go across the alley to Rudy's, looking for a handout from Mrs. Rudy who cooked in the small deli at the store and whose husband owned the business. There would be several places to visit because Queenie wanted the neighborhood to see Puppy after all this time and what a fine dog he had become. Right now, it was time to visit the doghouse to see if Soft Hands had brought food because Puppy was surely hungry and thirsty after his long trip.

Gidget remained laying half in and half out of the doghouse as Queenie and Puppy approached. Soft Hands had filled the water dish with fresh water, and the food dish was filled to the brim. Gidget had not made a move to either as she was well aware of the fact that Queenie would be making her way to both with Puppy, and if she were in the way, she would more than likely pay the price. And just as she had guessed, the queen and Puppy were on their way to the food. There was never enough food for Queenie and never had been. She was considerably overweight for a miniature dachshund, her belly almost dragging on the ground, and it had been that way ever since Gidget could remember. Queenie was the first puppy of a litter of seven little dachshunds, and Gidget the last, the runt. But it didn't really make that must difference to Gidget. She endured.

After Queenie and Puppy ate, they lay down for a nap, letting their meal settle, then they would be on their way, visiting, looking for treats, and going here and going there. What a magnificent time Queenie and Puppy would have, together again.

Gidget remained at the doghouse, not leaving her spot, looking at the food and water but giving no indication that she was interested in either even though she was quite hungry and thirsty not having had anything to eat or drink since last night. As was customary, Queenie always ate and drank first; and if there was anything left, then it was Gidget's turn. One could tell from her anorexic body what was left for her to eat. No matter, that was the way it had always been and probably always would be. Now that Puppy was here, would there ever be anything left for her to eat or drink? One could only guess.

The Memorial Day vacation would soon be over, but that made very little difference to Queenie and Puppy because each day was a great adventure. They had made the rounds of the neighborhood in addition to going to Rudy's across the alley and then visiting Sally and her little girls. They had ventured across the street to a vacant field filled with sagebrush and mice. What a treat that had been and a great meal. Puppy could hunt and dig exceptionally well, but why wouldn't he. After all, he was Queenie's one and only.

From the vacant field, Queenie started for the empty schoolyard as children were playing on the swings and slide even though school was out for the summer. The children immediately spotted Puppy and began to call him, wanting him to play, wanting to pet him and hold him. Queenie was unimpressed but did not mind that the children were so enamored with the little dog.

Tired of playing and on their way back to the doghouse, the children encouraged the dogs to stop at the motor home parked on the school grounds, and there the two dogs were instantly treated with meat leftovers and bread. The children from the motor home loved on Puppy again and again, giving little notice to Queenie, but that was all right with her because she didn't know the children so had not decided if she liked them or not. When Puppy was finally placed on the ground, Queenie started back toward home, and Puppy instantly followed. If the motor home and children were still there the next day, she and Puppy would probably return hoping for another meal of meat leftovers and bread.

When they returned home, Soft Hands had filled the dog bowls once again with fresh food and water. Queenie let Puppy eat right beside her, keeping a constant eye on Gidget, letting her know that she was not to come close until they were done; and if there wasn't anything left, well that would be too bad.

Before the holiday was over, Queenie wanted to show Puppy one of her very special places, one that Puppy had never enjoyed. At the edge of a hill not incredibly far from the doghouse, looking down on the river, Queenie lay down inviting Puppy to lay close to her. The sky was beginning to fill with the colors surrounding the setting sun, the evening becoming serene. There the two dogs, with ears perked up, could listen to the coyotes sing. For Queenie and Puppy, it was an ultimate joy.

III

Today would be the last day for fun and adventures for Queenie and Puppy as the long weekend was drawing to a close, and tomorrow, Boy would be returning home taking Puppy with him.

Queenie not knowing or caring that Puppy would be going proceeded to clean him up, licking, nuzzling, and loving on Puppy, knowing if he left, it would be awhile before he returned again. As it drew close to noon, Queenie and Puppy started their travels, making their way to the school to play with the children, and if the motor home was still there, maybe they would be treated to leftover meat and bread again.

Gidget lay in the opening of the doghouse, watching the two dogs make their way to the playground. She lay with her head on her paws, which was her general pose when left alone and, to her way of thinking, neglected. She had never been invited to go with the two dogs on their travels or to engage in any of their playful romps. Didn't Queenie or Puppy know that she loved Puppy? No, Queenie never gave her the chance. Wasn't she the one that dug Puppy out of the big blanket that engulfed him when he was born, and he could have been smothered? Wasn't she the one that licked, nudged, and moved Puppy to breathe and make his way to Queenie to nurse after he had been born? Puppy was loved double but had no opportunity to realize that because of Queenie. *The queen*! Gidget continued to lay there watching, just watching.

IV

As soon as they made their appearance, the children jumped out of the motor home to pet and play with Puppy. Wonderful treats were offered, and in no time, the two dogs were inside the motor home, the children petting, scratching, and playing with Puppy. Fresh treats were brought for Queenie, and after all of the rough and tumble, teasing, and playing, Puppy was placed on the couch which doubled as a bed with the children for a nap. Queenie was encouraged to lay on the floor on a blanket. What a wonderful time they were having and what an adventure.

Soon the motor home started up and moved away from the school playground, making its way to the highway and out of town, away from the doghouse, away from the Man, Soft Hands, and Boy and away from Gidget.

V

Queenie jumped awake as soon as she felt the rocking and swaying of the motor home stop. There they were, close to a gas pump and small restaurant. The surroundings did not appear familiar, but it did not matter, she smelled food, and it smelled good. As soon as the door of the motor home opened, Queenie tried to bound out but found herself falling down the steps of the motor home. Her big body and short legs simply could not maneuver the situation. Puppy was surely right behind her as he always followed without any hesitation. She made her way across the parking lot, following the delectable smell of the food. Making her way to the front door, she was pushed away so she made her way around to the back. Puppy was right there, she knew, but so taken with the smell of food that she did not check for sure.

At the back of the building was a small trash can, and there were a few specks of fresh bread and a small piece of hamburger which she immediately devoured. She felt thirsty and proceeded to make her way back to the front of the restaurant. Much to her dismay, the motor home was not there. She ran to the road, and there, running down the highway away from the small settlement, was the motor home, leaving her behind and, apparently, taking Puppy. *Taking Puppy!*

Queenie began running frantically after the motor home. *Don't take Puppy. Don't take Puppy! Please, don't take Puppy!* Oh, too soon she realized with her short legs and overweight body, she simply was no match for the motor home. She ran as far and as fast as she could, but simply there was no way to keep up. She stood there at the edge of the highway, barking and barking after the motor home, but it would not stop, and soon it was out of sight, rounding the corner far into the distance. Having been thirsty, she was far more in need of water now. She lay in the ditch next to the road, whimpering, crying, devastated that Puppy was gone, her one and only baby. She had been ever so proud of that dog. She had loved him with all her heart, and now he was gone, taken, and no way to find him or get him back.

VI

How long she lay in the small ditch next to the highway, she did not know, but it was becoming dark, and she was desperately in need of water. Where was she, she had no idea, but she did remember the restaurant and slowly made her way back, hoping to find something to drink.

It seemed like a long time before she finally found where the motor home had stopped, but there was no water to be found. Still out of breath and tired, she lay at the back door of the restaurant, but no one came out to offer her anything to drink or eat, so she simply lay there, wondering what she should do. It was becoming dark, and there was no doghouse to sleep in, no Soft Hands to fill the dog dish with food and water, and no Gidget.

Thirsty or not, she had to lay there at the back of the restaurant and rest. She lay there for a time, hoping that someone would open the backdoor, but no one did. She could sense water now that she took the time to smell the night air, and it wasn't long until she found a small pool of water in front of a small house, and it was relatively fresh being fed from the hose watering the lawn in front of the home. Queenie was so thirsty she lapped and lapped the water even if it was in the middle of the road.

She made her way back under the steps at the back-door of the restaurant and tried to make herself comfortable. The ground was rocky and damp, and the night air was almost cold, but there did not seem to be much choice. If only she was back at the doghouse with the long green shag carpeting, with plenty to eat, clean water to drink, and Gidget to lay close to her, keeping her cozy and warm. The thought would not leave her. Who would be so mean and thoughtless as to take her away from her home, take Puppy, and leave her somewhere that was totally unfamiliar and perhaps hostile. A feeling of utter despair began to roll over her like a cold wind from the north.

VII

Gidget had stayed in the doghouse almost all day, watching across the yard to the school playground where Queenie and Puppy had gone that morning. The motor home was now gone, and so it appeared that Queenie and Puppy were out romping around the neighborhood, having totally forgotten about Gidget, which really did not surprise her at all. The two dogs had been gone almost all day, which was surprising because Queenie was always searching for food, and if none was to be found, she would be right back to the doghouse as the food bowl was almost always full.

As the afternoon turned into evening, Gidget still remained at the doghouse, watching. Gidget continued to watch until the sun sank behind the mountains, and it started to get dark. The Boy and his dad had returned from fishing and were excited about their catch. Gidget could hear the noise inside the house as preparations were being made to "fry the fish." No one came to see if Queenie and Puppy had returned, and the food bowl was full as was the water bowl, so there was no need. It was surprising that Boy had not come to check on his dog. There was too much excitement inside the house over the fishing trip.

Gidget got backed into the doghouse as the air was beginning to cool off, and even though she was Queenie's blanket, Queenie kept her warm too. Gidget knew that Queenie would come home. She and Puppy must have been having lots of fun and had ventured far enough away that showing up before dark would not be possible. Surely, they would appear before morning.

VIII

Gidget lay slightly inside the doghouse, waiting. She really did not think much of sleeping because the night air was quite cool, and her warm pillow was not available. Her ears were up, listening, knowing that Queenie and Puppy would show up at any moment. Somehow the night slipped away, and the two dogs were still nowhere to be seen.

It was daylight, Gidget had a quick drink and prepared to venture across the street to the playground where the motor home had been. Perhaps Queenie and Puppy had found a comfortable place to sleep and decided not to go back to the doghouse. But what were they doing for food? That was one thing that definitely would bring Queenie back to the doghouse, knowing there would always be something to eat there.

Gidget trotted slowly with her nose to the ground, smelling, smelling, trying to distinguish Queenie's smell from all the others that were available. She did find a small trail, but it stopped short right next to the edge of the playground. Gidget continued to look and smell across one side of the playground then back again, but the two dogs were nowhere to be found. The only thing to do was to go back to the doghouse and wait. They would surely be coming home, and tomorrow, the Man would be taking Boy back to his home, and Puppy would be going too. Then things would finally be back to normal.

Gidget returned to the doghouse and slowly backed in like she always did, half in and half out with her head resting on her paws. She watched the playground across from the house intently, knowing that the two dogs would show up before nightfall. Soon, the sun was beginning to set behind the mountains, but the two dogs still had not returned. Somehow Gidget wanted to howl in grief because she was lonely, lonely without Queenie to lay next to, lonely without her short snarl that would remind her not to eat or drink until Queenie was done, lonely because Queenie just was not there.

IX

Queenie heard the backdoor of the restaurant open and someone making their way to the garbage can. There was this delightful smell of something to eat, and her ears and nose were right in tune with the steps of the garbage approaching the container. She could hear the sack being emptied into the can, then retreat back inside.

She made her way to the garbage can, circling, trying to find a way to retrieve a meal, but that was not going to be possible. There was no way to tip the can over, to find some way to get anything out of the bottom. It was totally impossible, and the smell of food was almost overwhelming. She lay there beginning to feel nauseous. Her stomach was totally empty and had been since morning. She lay down next to the can and began to whimper. It wasn't long before she dozed off. It was becoming a very long hard day.

Startled awake, Queenie made her way back under the stairs desperate for some comfort concerning the dilemma she was in. Food was always on her mind and always had been, and here all of a sudden there was none.

As she lay dozing, her nose began to twitch, and her ears became alert. There was something moving close to the garbage can, and she could hear and smell it, and it smelled good. She lay very still then moved like a flash, devouring the mouse that was about to begin invading the garbage can. How delightful to her very empty stomach. At last, there was something there to nourish her, and now she could rest and wonder what tomorrow would bring.

X

Gidget lay watching the playground most of the evening, dozing off on occasion then awakening, suddenly hoping that Queenie and Puppy would be returning but to no avail. Morning came, and neither dog had made their appearance.

Apparently, Soft Hands and the Man had not realized that neither of the two dogs were at the doghouse, and the Boy was making ready to return home. Soft Hands was calling Queenie, but there was no response. The Man was looking and calling, and the Boy was calling, but no dogs were showing up. Both the Man and the Boy started to comb the neighborhood calling, searching for the two dogs. The Boy was beginning to cry that he could not leave without Puppy. The situation was becoming tense, and Gidget could feel the frustration, but there was nothing that could be done. Both dogs were gone, and it became apparent that neither were going to be found. Gidget looked at the full dog dish but had no appetite. The food had not been touched, and if Queenie and Puppy had been around at all, the dog dish would be empty. Finally, the Man consoled the Boy and assured him that when the dogs showed up, the Man would bring Puppy to him. Everyone was tearful when they said their goodbyes.

When the Man and the Boy left, Gidget once more left the doghouse and crossed the street to the playground. She searched again for any scent of Queenie but found no more than what she had when she made her first trip to where the motor home had been. Returning to the doghouse, she again lay barely peering out with her head resting on her paws.

XI

Queenie only dozed for a short time, then hunger and thirst set in again. It was dark with hardly any moon, but it made no difference. She could make her way just fine, but the question was, Which way to go, and was this place to be her newfound home?

She remembered where she had found water before and made her way in that direction. Even though it was a mud puddle that had developed from a lawn being overwatered, it made no difference. She quenched her thirst and proceeded on. This was definitely not a large town, but for an overweight dog with short legs, it was still difficult to go from house to house thinking she might find something familiar. For some reason, she kept thinking she would run onto the doghouse, but the directions were fuzzy, everything was strange, and she could not find it. She did, however, smell food and made her way toward it. A lone water bowl and dog dish full of food were set on the ground next to the steps leading into someone's home. What luck! Not needing water, she emptied the food bowl, crawled under the steps, made a warm nest in the grass and weeds underneath, and immediately fell fast asleep.

It was barely becoming light when she awoke, no Gidget lying next to her, keeping her warm, and the air was chilled. She checked the food bowl just in case it may have been filled again, but it was empty. Feeling secure, she crawled back under the porch steps and proceeded back to her nest when the backdoor opened, and a woman's voice began calling. Queenie could hear the two bowls being picked up as the woman was calling and calling. Whatever was she calling, Queenie did not know, but then it happened—she was spotted.

The porch steps squeaked as the woman ran into the house and then out again, with a broom in hand. Pushing the broom in underneath the steps, she began beating Queenie and yelling for her to get out. Queenie made a mad dash as fast as her rotund body would carry her, trying hard to dodge the broom and then the handle. Smacked across the back once or twice, Queenie was yelping and crying, running away from the woman as fast as she could go. She made it into the roadway and continued as fast as she could back to the restaurant. At the time, it was to be the safest place to go.

The steps coming out of the back of the restaurant had a small space that Queenie could fit into. It wasn't the doghouse by any means, but the steps did provide some cover and protection. It would also provide some shade during the heat of the day. She lay there for quite a while, her stomach rumbling from hunger, but she remained, still trying to figure out where she was and wondering why she could not find her way home to the doghouse and Gidget.

As the day wore on, Queenie remained under the steps, venturing out only as the sun began to go down. Feeling more secure under the cover of darkness, Queenie again began to look for food and water. There had not been any mice around the restaurant; otherwise, she probably would have stayed close to her hideaway. Again, she ventured to where she had found food and water outside in a bowl, and hopefully, the broom lady would be in the house. Much to her delight, there was some food left in the bowl, and the bowl with the water was full. She ate what was in the bowl and emptied the bowl of water. There would be no way that she would stay under these steps again, fearing that the broom would be after her even if it was dark.

Feeling somewhat fed, she felt compelled to start exploring and maybe find the doghouse. There was little activity in this settlement except for whatever was going on at the restaurant, so there was no worry about lots of traffic. Queenie set her nose in the air but could smell little else than the night air. It was cool, which was nice, so she set her nose close to the ground, her ears alert, and started off.

XII

How many days had come and gone and how many times had she started out in the evening with her nose close to the ground, her ears alert, looking, looking, looking, and finding nothing she did not know. She had hardly enough food to satisfy her hunger, barely enough water to keep her hydrated, chased away with a broom, yelled at, told to get away, sprayed with a hose, and even little kids threw rocks at her, and worst of all, there was no doghouse to be found and no Gidget. Her home had become the damp ground under the steps going out of the back door of the restaurant, and never did anyone find it necessary to throw her a small bit to eat.

Of course, she had no collar and no dog license, so she must be some kind of stray dog no one wanted or cared about. Worst of all, she did not know where she was and how to find her way back to Gidget and the doghouse. One more time, she would venture out when it became dark, hoping against hope to find something familiar or at least something good to eat. A feeling of despair was beginning to consume her.

XIII

Gidget lay half in and half out of the doghouse in her regular pose, front feet out in front where she rested her head. Her gaze was always the same, straight across the street at the school playground, hoping against all hope that Queenie and Puppy would come bounding across the street straight to the bowl full of food.

Each day since Queenie and Puppy had left, Gidget ventured out but never at the same time each day, always making a round of the places she thought Queenie would frequent when she had been at the doghouse.

First, she would go to Peterson's across the street, then up the block to the trailer park. Gidget would take considerable time there because there were several places to check on since several families lived there, and Queenie always enjoyed the attention she received from the children at the park. Then down the block to Coopers, then next door to Rudy's, the small grocery store, deli, and gas station. Queenie always visited the grocery store because Mrs. Rudy always fed her something, pieces of bread and maybe some of her wonderful roast beef, and then on to Sally's. Sally always let Queenie inside to play with her little girls, and after Puppy came to visit, Sally would let him come in too. She had never let Gidget in because Gidget had never been allowed to go with Queenie.

The results of the journey were always the same, no Queenie and no Puppy. It was becoming tiresome to make the search, but Gidget was lost, totally lost without Queenie. Even if her relationship with Queenie had been difficult, she could not help but love her, and she knew that Queenie in her own way loved her too.

Finding nothing, she returned to the doghouse, had a small lap of water, and lay down in the door again to watch the ants crawl in and out of the food bowl, carrying the dog food to their underground storage to be consumed during the winter. She might have one bite of food, but she simply had no appetite. Soft Hands would, on occasion, lift her up and pet her warmly, asking why she did not eat. Gidget had been small and frail, to begin with, but as the summer wore on, she was becoming almost intolerably thin. Her backbone was beginning to protrude, her little ribs were beginning to show, and her eyes, her eyes were so sad. Soft Hands was at a loss as to how to comfort the little dog. She cooed to her in a kind, gentle voice, telling Gidget that she knew she missed Queenie and wished that she was still there with her in the doghouse, but it did no good.

XIV

Queenie started out during the late afternoon since the day was somewhat cool. It wasn't hard to find some water as several lawns had become dry, and the sprinklers were running. She drank at one sprinkler until her thirst was satisfied. This was the first time in a while she had had enough water to drink. It made her feel much better and a little more adventurous.

She took her time looking for something to eat, went back to the restaurant to recheck the garbage can, and found, to her surprise, a piece of hamburger that had fallen to the ground. She was feeling good about the evening. There was no wind, no traffic up and down the few streets in town, and no children playing outside to make things noisy. Maybe things were beginning to look up for her hunt.

Queenie's senses were alert. Her nose was to the ground, ears up, and eyes sharp. She really was enjoying this stroll when she caught it, the smell of food; whatever kind, it made no difference, but it smelled so good. She was almost overwhelmed with the rumbling this smell created in her shrunken stomach and the smell was overwhelming her caution. She started running as fast as her short legs would take her in the direction of this delectable aroma, her nose staying low to the ground.

All at once, she was there; and there, right in front of her, was a dish full of wonderful soft dog food, something she had not experienced for what seemed to be a long, long time. She was so hungry for this delicacy she could not gulp it down fast enough, and then it happened. At first, the growl was very low but slowly became more intense. She barely had time to adjust herself when the attack came. The dog wasn't much bigger than she was, but she had invaded its space and its food dish. That could not be allowed, and the other dog was about to set things straight.

It attacked Queenie from the side, its jaws setting hard into her neck skin, but she was quick enough not to allow the skin to be torn, rolling to her side, dislodging the jaws; but the fight was definitely on. The dog lunged again, and when it did, Queenie went for the chest; but the dog didn't back down, ripping into her ear. Still, she was a badger dog, and that instinct was kicking in, and she wasn't backing down either.

It didn't take long, and Queenie had her way with the other dog, leaving a gash in its chest and hindquarters and injuring the back leg in a bad way. She managed to finish the food she hadn't been allowed to eat, then started back for the steps behind the restaurant. She was hurting, but at least for the first time in quite a while, she had had enough water to drink and had a full stomach.

XV

Queenie lay under the steps for some time, licking the wounds she could get to. The dog fight had caused her great distress even though she had more to eat and drink today than she had had since being abandoned in this settlement; she was totally exhausted. Not only that, she hardly felt like she had had good food and water for a change. No doubt, she was a badger dog, but she had never fought another dog or another animal of any kind for that matter, and it had taken a toll on her. Yes, she ruled the roost with Gidget, but she only had to look and growl at her, and Gidget did just what she was supposed to. That was not the case this time. She lay her head on her paws to rest and was soon asleep.

She lay under the steps for some time. How many days, she did not know, and it did not matter. Her body was sore, and she continued to lick the open wounds that she could reach. There was a real need for water and something to eat again, but that task seemed almost too much to accomplish. Another day and she would venture out, this time during the morning, and hopefully, she would not again encounter that dog. She was determined, though, if she did, the results would be the same. She would not back down. She closed her eyes and fell back asleep.

It wasn't long, and the stairs above her creaked, and she knew right away that the garbage from the kitchen was being taken to the trash. She waited quietly until the dishwasher walked back up the stairs, into the restaurant, and closed the door. Queenie then made an exit from what served as her doghouse and trotted to the garbage can, hoping that not all of the garbage had made it into the can, that something had fallen out, and that she might be able to make a meal but to no avail.

She was hungry and thirsty but did not really know if she had the desire to start searching the settlement again for a place to get a drink or something to eat. But the situation was becoming dire, so she started out again. She checked at the same places she had numerous times before during her stay in this place. Her stomach no longer was so close to the ground that it almost drug in the dirt. She was no longer so overweight for a miniature dachshund. Even so, she did not seem to have the energy or the strength that she once had. It was the same routine, and she did find water but nothing to eat, which was no surprise. Then she thought again. Should she, or shouldn't she? The hunger was gnawing away at her, and she had to make a decision. She decided that one more time should not make a difference. The dog that had tried to discourage her had been thoroughly intimidated or should have been, so she decided to go back to where her last meal had been. Risky, true, but her hunger was almost overtaking her and now in control.

The food dish came into sight, and, happy day, it was full; and there was no dog around. She made a beeline for the dish and could not consume the dog food fast enough. She was enjoying the meal so much that she failed to hear the sound of footsteps behind her until it was too late. Queenie felt a quick pain in her side as she flew through the air. The man's steel-toed boot caught her straight in the rib cage, and the kick made her fly through the air like a punted football. She righted herself as she hit the ground out of breath but bolted away from the man as fast as her short legs would take her. She couldn't help but make a muffled cry as she ran for her makeshift doghouse. Fortunately, he did not follow her, but she could hear him hollering at her at the top of his lungs.

She lay under the steps behind the restaurant and whimpered at the pain in her side, trying to catch a full breath. She was in pain again.

Once again, she was hurt, not just physically but also wondering if she was ever to escape this situation. As she lay there, the day slipped by; and as the sun set over the mountains, a decision had to be made. She had to find her way home. She had to find her way back to the doghouse, to her home, to where she belonged, where she was cared for and about, and to her friend.

XVI

In the cool of the morning, Queenie made her way to the ridge of the hill at the edge of the settlement, and even though her side was still painful, it made no difference. Before her lay a valley filled with fields lush and green. The smell of the mountain hay, the orchard grass, the clover, and the bromegrass filled the air, the river was surrounded by blue spruce and aspen trees, and the fields were now being watered. Why had she stayed in this settlement so long? Why hadn't she started out to find her home? She could not remain here and survive. A decision had to be made even if it might not be the right one, and the outcome would be dire. "Gidget, I'm coming. I'm coming home!"

She was on her way, and there was an excitement in her that had not been there until today. Instinctively, she started in the direction that the sun had gone down, not really knowing for certain that this way was right but just knowing somehow that it was.

Even though she was not nearly as heavy as she had been, her short legs did not cover a lot of ground, and it took time to go any distance from the small town. Traveling in the shallow ditch next to the highway was probably not the fastest route, but it kept her safe from all of the summer tourist traffic. As the day began to heat up, she paused to rest, just long enough to cool off a bit in the tall grass then continue on. It took awhile, but she knew she was next to a field, and she could sense the water running through it. She began to wonder why she had not found this place before.

As she made her way under the barbwire fence, she caught the smell and could hear something to eat. Of course, there was never a time that Queenie did not have an appetite, and fortunately, a mouse was to be had. The mouse was gathering on a ditch bank, and the ditch was full of water. There were no people, and there were no dogs. A secure place to find food and water. This was wonderful!

After she had eaten and had a good drink, she returned to the shallow ditch next to the road, found some tall grass, and napped through the heat of the day. As evening advanced, she continued on. When hungry, she slipped under the barbwire fence, had a drink, found a mouse, ate her fill, slipped back to the shallow ditch next to the road, rested, and then continued on. How long this routine would last, she did not know; but hopefully, it would continue until she found Gidget.

XVII

Her travels were going well, and she continued to puzzle why she had not left the town sooner and begun the trip to find Gidget. Perhaps it was because, in the back of her mind, Puppy would return, and the two would be together, and that would be enough. However, it made no difference now because Puppy was gone, probably forever, and she had to make it back to the doghouse.

Queenie noticed that the sky began to darken, and suddenly there was a loud cracking sound and then a rumble that seemed to shake the ground. This continued for a time as the sky became darker and darker, and then suddenly, it began to rain heavily. Then small balls of ice began to pelt her on the back and sides. Where to find cover from the storm? There simply was nothing in sight that would afford her protection. She began to run as fast as her short legs would take her, out of the ditch next to the road, into the field, and up a small hill; and when reaching the top, she spotted what looked to be some kind of stack of something she had never seen before, but maybe it would provide the shelter she was looking for.

The big hay bales were stacked close to one another but not too tight and did have a gap or two in between the lower bales where Queenie could back into out of the weather. It was dry and warm, and she was away from the storm. As she lay there, she felt secure. It made no matter what was happening outside, let it rain. This was more like the doghouse but no Gidget keeping her warm.

XVIII

The haystack was a wonderful place to be, warm and secure. She lay in between the bales, watching the rain and hail pour down, totally unaffected. It would be over soon, but until then, she would lay sheltered when her eyes closed, and she was soon sound asleep.

When she finally woke, the rain and hail had quit; but night had come, and the sky was quite dark, with no visible clouds, no moon, and no stars. Lightning still flashed across the sky and thunder could be heard off in the distance as the storm had moved to the east. Queenie felt more secure than she had for quite some time. The ground was dry and soft, and the interior warm and cozy. She began reminiscing about the doghouse, and when she had laid at the door watching the nighttime sky, the stars, the moon, and Gidget laying close by. Her side still gave her some pain, but she felt more content and secure than she had for quite some time.

XIX

The morning sun was beginning to fill the sky when Queenie finally woke. She was well-rested and eager to start again when a long-haired black-and-white dog made its appearance right in front of her, up close and personal. It lay its head on its front paws in a crouching position while the back legs held the vigorously wagging tail standing straight up. The dog was much larger than Queenie but appeared to be quite young and, upon seeing Queenie, began to dance around, then run in a circle, jump, and bark. It was most definitely wanting to play which was something Queenie had never done.

Queenie lay there watching the dog, puzzled as to what to make of all the activity. The dog came close, and Queenie was tempted to give it the old curled lip snarl like the one she would give Gidget but decided against it, watching in amazement. The dog lay on the ground in front of her then jumped up and bound toward her, then stopped and lay down, then jumped up again and began running in a circle. Queenie began to move out from her shelter, and the dog trotted right up to her then suddenly ran ahead then waited for Queenie to catch up. Finally, it dawned on Queenie that maybe all this activity might be fun, and began running the best her short legs would take her, chasing the dog, then laying down, waiting for the dog to make its move.

Soon, the two dogs were in a tussle, running, jumping on each other, rolling in the dirt, and playing dog tag. Queenie was thoroughly enjoying the company of the black-and-white dog and was having more fun than she had ever had.

After some time, the dogs stopped for a rest when the black-and-white dog perked up its ears and began to make its way back to the haystack. Someone was whistling, and the dog was returning to the whistle. Queenie followed but at a much slower pace. She stood there watching as the dog jumped into the back of a pickup, which then pulled out of the driveway onto the highway. Suddenly, the dog she had been having so much fun with was gone. She lay there trying to gather her thoughts somewhat in dismay after all the activity then finally deciding it must be time to continue on as there was no need to go back to the haystack. Assessing her surroundings, the scene had changed. There were no hayfields or pasture, and she was not sure if she should make her way back to the highway or proceed under the barbwire fence and into the sagebrush field. The river was close, so there would be easy access to water making the decision easier.

Avoiding the house, the driveway, and the main highway, Queenie crawled under the barbwire fence and trotted into the sagebrush forest.

The scenery was completely different from what she had been used to. The sagebrush was so much taller than she was there was barely any way to find which way she should go. The ground was firm, though, with no sharp stubble to irritate her paws, and the fragrance around the sagebrush was ever so soothing. Queenie continued on, hoping she would be able to find her way.

X X

The days were warm and the nights still cool, so the travel was going well, and she didn't feel the need to stop and rest and perhaps nap and cool off as often as she had. This was going to be a good day, and she would make time. She felt confident that it would not be long before she would find Gidget and the doghouse. The thought of the excitement she would feel when all of this was over was almost overwhelming. It is what kept her going, never giving in or giving up. She was a badger dog, aggressive, relentless. She was built to persist, a hunter, a hunter of badgers. And badgers were one of the most fearless and aggressive animals on earth, so what did that say about her? Yes, she was feeling good.

She could hear water running, and it wasn't far, and she could really use a drink; then suddenly, it was there in front of her, a river and a big one, with lots of water. It appeared to be going in the same direction that she was, so why not get a good drink and travel close by. There surely would be other animals making their way to the water for a drink just like her. So that would mean water and perhaps something to eat.

She took a good drink and continued on. The rocks on the bank were too hurtful to the pads on her feet, so she distanced herself slightly from the river where the ground was harder, and she could make better time. If the terrain remained the same, and the travel was as good as this, she would find the doghouse in no time. When she did take time to rest, she would find good shelter under one of the sage brush. There might even be a small bit of grass to lay on.

XXI

Travel was easy now. She was close to water; there were no mice, but there were ground squirrels which were much better. Even if they would make a mad dash for cover, she was, after all, a badger dog and could dig as fast and as hard as any ground squirrel.

One day blended into the next, and how long she had been away from the small settlement, she did not know or care for that matter. She was sure that she was headed in the right direction, and it would only be a matter of time before she would be home. She would tolerate the hot sun, the cool nights, the wind, and rain, if it rained. No matter what, she would continue on.

Making her way under a barbed-wire fence, the ground on the other side changed to an irrigated field. The grass was wet, but the water was not incredibly deep. This situation slowed her travel, and not only that, she was moving farther away from the river; but as long as she could remain in this field, there would be water. Regardless, she continued on across the field, feeling confident she was headed in the right direction.

There appeared to be a procession of wire fences, each field being different from the previous one. Again, Queenie made her way under another fence, finding the ground's soft grass and some short stubble slowing her travels, causing the pads on her feet to receive an occasional poke. Hopefully, this wouldn't cause a problem. She stopped for a rest, licking the pads on her feet, hoping to ease some of the tenderness. Regardless, she had to rest. Maybe she would nap for just a while and then continue on which is exactly what she did.

She was abruptly awakened when the wind began to blow hard; the thunder began to sound overhead, and once again, rain began to pelt down on her. She began hurriedly searching for shelter, but there were no trees, sagebrush, or bushes, nothing that she could hide in or under. She began frantically running to find something because now the rain was coming in a torrent. There right in front of her was a hole in the side of the road bank, back under the barbed-wire fence and into the hole which turned out to be a large metal pipe.

Out of the rain, she shook herself off and proceeded forward. She smelled something peculiar but paid little attention. She wasn't concerned because she was safely out of the weather. And then, she saw what the smell was all about, and she was not about to share the space with another animal. In her aggressive and combative badger dog way with a curled lip and barred teeth, she made a run at the creature that was there in the pipe with her. As she was quickly making her way toward the animal, the black-and-white tail immediately went into the air, and then it happened, the spray hit her square in the face. Queenie froze, unable to move, then with a high-pitched cry turned and raced out of the pipe as though shot from a canon.

The skunk, knowing full well the damage it had inflicted, strolled smugly to the edge of the pipe opening, its black-and-white tail standing straight in the air. When at the edge of the pipe before stepping onto the ground, the skunk lifted its nose skyward, taking a good, deep breath of the freshly washed air then stepped daintily down onto the embankment and slowly waddled off to its next destination.

Queenie was in terrible distress. Her eyes were burning beyond belief; she was gasping for air, the spray having entered her nose and mouth, making its way quickly down her throat into her lungs, setting everything on fire. Taking in a breath was short of impossible and, when accomplished, drew the spray deeper into her lungs. She could not see but managed to make it down off the embankment, under the barbed-wire fence, and into the rain-soaked pasture. She lay there trying to regain some kind of bearing then began to slither through the wet grass like a snake, doing everything she could imagine to try and remove the stench that surrounded every part of her being.

Having no idea where she really was in the field, she tried opening her eyes, but it simply was too difficult. Even if she had been able to, everything would have been a blur. The only thing she could do was to remain where she was, roll and slither, try to wash her eyes with the wet grass, and wait, which was something she simply was not wanting to do. And then there was the matter of trying to get a decent breath which was even more difficult. She finally chewed a large mouth full of the wet grass and swallowed, which helped to relieve some of the incredible burnings in her throat. Exhausted, Queenie lay in the rain-soaked grass, panting and fitfully wondering how or if she would ever recover.

XXII

Travel the last few days had been good. The water and food had been relatively easy to find; there had only been one dog, and it had been friendly and fun but now this. She was in agony. How was she going to be able to survive what had just happened? Would she ever be able to find the doghouse now? Queenie continued to lay in the wet pasture exhausted. Her eyes were closed, stinging and beginning to water, and her breathing had somewhat recovered, but it was impossible to take a good deep breath. There was no choice but to stay exactly where she was, hoping this would all go away.

Under any other circumstances, her appetite would be running wild, but she was not one bit hungry. The fact of the matter was she had totally forgotten about food. Right now, she felt very vulnerable, not knowing exactly where she was in the field. Crawling along on her belly, she bumped something hard. Maybe a rock, sagebrush, a fence post? Whatever it was, she moved in close so that she could really feel it, making her feel more secure.

She shook her head, putting her paws back over her eyes, and just lay there, immobile, waiting. How many hours, how many days would she have to wait for the burning to go away and her eyes to see again? It was an enormous question. She just lay there because there was nothing else to do.

XXIII

Gidget lay half in and half out of the doghouse with her head on her paws, which was her general position. Rarely did she leave now after having made so many rounds of the neighborhood, always thinking that she would eventually find Queenie and possibly Puppy. Why she would even bother was a mystery. Queenie had hardly ever had time for her, and about the only occasion that she did, it was with a curled lip and set sharp teeth. Yes, Queenie was *the queen*, and she never let Gidget forget that fact.

As the summer continued, she had grown thinner and thinner, watching the ants carry her food into their underground winter storage. On occasion, she would have a bite or two, which is what Queenie would have allowed; but her appetite, what little she had ever had, was almost nonexistent.

Today, maybe she would take a different route but cover the same territory, as usual, going to Rudy's, then the trailer park and if she were really adventuresome, maybe over to the school grounds. Then again, maybe she would save her energy and just remain at the doghouse. Giving a short sigh, she decided on the latter, making a move clear to the back of the doghouse, and looked out of the opening, which gave her a clear view of the small fence that surrounded most of the backyard.

XXIV

Queenie continued laying close to the post or the rock whatever it was and began somewhat to regain a little of her ability to take a decent breath and even thought that perhaps some vision was beginning to return. Her eyes were still watering which was probably helping the situation, but recovering from this simply was not happening fast enough. How many days she had been here was hard to determine. It seemed she had laid there for a long time but didn't know for certain because she couldn't distinguish between night and day, but it hardly made any difference because she wasn't going anywhere until she could see.

Getting by without being able to get a good smell of what was around her was one thing, but not being able to see was quite another. She felt certain that her eyesight would return along with being able to take a good, deep breath and being able to smell, but in the meantime, she just lay there. For the first time, probably ever, she could feel the wind blow a cool, soft breeze. She could hear a bird chirping somewhere and some insect making a strange, unfamiliar sound.

She was beginning to get a sense of loneliness and longing, and it was beginning to overtake her. If she were at the doghouse, there would be help, and that help would be Gidget. She would lick the pads on Queenie's feet to take the soreness out, she would lick Queenie's eyes to help them heal, and she would lay very close to Queenie to keep her warm which was something she always did. Gidget was always there thinking first of Queenie and then maybe herself. She did bark too much, but that didn't mean anything now.

Queenie had always been proud of the fact that she was a "badger dog." Her registered name was Queenie Luitgard, named for German royalty. She had never really treated Gidget with that respect, being a "badger dog," but she was exactly that a "badger dog." They were out of the same litter, her registered name was Gisela Richenza, and yes, she was named for German royalty too. Pondering that realization for a time, she began to feel some encouragement, somehow knowing instinctively that her eyes would heal along with her sense of smell and being able to take a good, long breath without anything stinging and that she would make it back to the doghouse and Gidget.

XXV

She could definitely use a good drink of water helping to put out some of the fire she was still feeling in her mouth and throat. Not being able to see or to really smell, the water was becoming a big hurdle to make it over right now. The field had dried some, and there did not seem to be any obvious puddles to drink from and no wet grass. She could hear the river and somehow had to make it there. It had never been that far away; that she was certain of, but right now wasn't exactly sure what direction to go. Maybe if she just tried to find a little puddle of water, she could survive for a bit longer. The field had been quite wet, and just maybe not everything was dry. Without moving far from her comfort zone, she managed to find a small puddle and though it didn't totally satisfy her thirst and tasted like mud it helped.

Her eyes were still not healed, but she felt she could make out some of her surroundings. The burning was beginning to diminish somewhat. She rolled in the grass, but that really did not help how she smelled. That smell, maybe that was the reason she couldn't determine what was around her because her nose was overwhelmed by the pungent odor. One more day and hopefully she could be on her way.

The evening was coming on, and hunger was beginning to get the better of her. As the sun was beginning to set behind the mountains, she felt certain that she could make out enough of the terrain to start for the river, and maybe, just maybe along the way, she would hear or smell a mouse or maybe a ground squirrel. Anything would do about now, maybe even a grasshopper.

She felt certain that having a drink of good fresh water, washing her eyes, and having a good roll on the wet ground or even in the shallow river water would help her sense of smell and her eyes to make a comeback and that she could start her travels again. The sun had not fully set, so there still was some light. She started out, moving very slowly and deliberately.

The ground was somewhat soft, and traveling was fairly easy. Her breathing remained a problem, and she was forced to stop and rest and catch her breath. It was almost dark when she finally reached the river's edge and immediately made her way slightly into the water. She lapped the fresh, cool water ferociously then rolled on the muddy bank hopeful it would help to clean her hair and diminish the smell she was going to be forced to carry with her.

Finding a clump of grass under a bush, she circled to make a nest and then proceeded to rest. She was regaining strength, her eyes continued to water, and her sight was returning. Perhaps one more night then in the morning, she would feel confident and strong enough to start again.

XXVI

She was making some time and was not far from the river, so water was not a problem, and so far, there had been something to eat. There had not been any obstacles that she couldn't conquer even if she was somewhat disabled, so she had been making what she thought was a fairly good time. Following the river made her feel secure, and it was apparently going in the same direction she thought she should be going.

Suddenly, without notice, the river was moving out of sight; there was no bank to follow, and there in front of her was a very steep hill. She sat pondering what to do. Did she have the strength? She sat assessing her options and then decided the only way was to climb up. That was exactly what she intended to do. It was with considerable determination and effort that she made her way up the incline and then climbed onto a wooden slab. Looking left and then right down a long line of steel rails, she mustered all of her strength and, then with all her might, jumped up onto the rail; but her short legs would not allow her to make it all the way over. Trying to push with her hind legs, she almost became stuck on the top of this thing but finally pushed hard enough that the front of her body fell over the rail so that she could grab the wood with her front claws and pull her body totally over the rest of the way.

It was exhausting, but she got the job done. Looking ahead, she saw exactly the same situation right in front of her. Well, she had made it one time, and she was sure she could do it again. As she made her way to the steel rail, she began to feel a tremble in the wood she was standing on, and she could hear what seemed to sound like a *click, click, click* along the rail. Not having experienced anything like this before, she became alarmed and raced to the rail, jumping with all of her might to try and make it over without wasting time. She just about made it and was able to grab the wood on the other side with her long claws and, without any hesitation, pulled herself over, running down the embankment as the ground was beginning to tremble more and more. It didn't take long, and the train, making a frightful noise, passed her as she lay tight to the ground until it ran by. When it was gone, the ground became still again. She lay there for a while, trying to take long, deep breaths. At this point, taking any breath was still difficult, and only short breaths seemed to be the best way to calm herself. Eventually, she was able to regain her composure and continued on.

XXVII

She followed a small gully that ran between the railroad bed and another steep hill. Knowing she was becoming farther and farther from the river, it would make it harder for her to find water, or she would have to somehow make the trip back to find the river, and she was not about to do that. It was a difficult choice, but she decided to make it up the steep hill to the highway.

The pads on her feet were becoming quite sore, but she wasn't about to stop until she made it to the top. It had taken most of the day to get where she was, and even though it would be dark soon, she was determined to continue on. There had been several days of convalescing, and she had to try her best to make up time.

When she left the settlement, the road had been like this one. It was smooth, and she could easily trot on the surface. There had been traffic on the other one, but she generally could hear and feel whatever was there and get out of the way as it sped by. The small ditch next to the road was just like the one that she had laid in when the motor home had taken Puppy and where she had been abandoned. This was familiar, and she felt all right about it. The days were still warm, but the nights were cooler, which should be making travel easier. She trotted down the road, close to the edge, wanting to make sure that if a car was coming, she would have adequate time to make it into the ditch alongside.

Pushing herself to make time and distance was working for her. Queenie trotted down the pavement as fast as her short legs would allow. There was no traffic on this road at this time, making it much easier for her not having to move back and forth from the road to the ditch and vice versa. Besides, this smooth surface was much easier on the pads of her feet.

XXVIII

Traveling at night was easy and fast being that there was little traffic on the road, and if the moon was up, it was fairly easy to sense what the surrounding area was about. Occasionally, there would be some night sounds, and there were lots of stars if the sky was clear.

This night was quite still as she made her way down the middle of the highway. The moon was bright, and the sky was clear, allowing the stars to totally expose their twinkle. Queenie sat still for a moment, wondering about night sounds. For one reason or another, she had not really taken a lot of time to sit and listen at night and how soothing it could be. How wonderful it would be to hear the coyotes sing if there were any around. She sat still, hoping maybe there would be a *yip, yip, yip* and then *ohwoo, ohwoo,* but there was only stillness. Suddenly, there was a sound, loud and roaring, a truck racing down the road straight for her as she sat in the center of the road. She raced to the edge, down the small embankment, to the small ditch next to the road. Safely making down the incline as the truck raced by, she stepped hard, and a sharp piece of stubble stabbed the soft skin surrounding the pad on her paw. This wasn't just a scratch; blood began to flow, and there was no indication it would stop any time soon.

Once again, she was hurt; but this time, she could see, breathe, and smell much better and would be disabled only long enough to lick the wound and stop the bleeding and then would be on her way.

XXIX

G idget lay in her regular repose, half in and half out of the doghouse door, maintaining vigilance of the schoolyard, ever hoping that Queenie would make an appearance at some point in time.

She had decided early on that it was of hardly any use to search the neighborhood for Queenie and perhaps Puppy, but maybe today she would venture out as it had been quite some time since she had even thought about leaving the doghouse, and just maybe today would be the day she would find Queenie. There was always hope, and that is what Gidget had to hang on to.

Starting down the alley behind the doghouse, not stopping to check at Sally's and knowing too that there was little need to stop and visit Mrs. Rudy as anytime she had been at the backdoor of the store, no one came with any treats, and she eventually just left. However, the wonderful aroma of the deli meat cooking in the outdoor oven made it ever so hard to simply walk away, but that is just what she did.

The trailer park seemed the most likely place where Queenie might be as someone might be keeping her inside or secured out of sight, and that was why Gidget could not find her. There were several places to search, and as soon as Gidget reached the edge of the park, her nose was on the ground seeking any scent that might solve this mystery. She was instantly busy trying to distinguish everything she was smelling when she suddenly heard a low, guttural growl, not unlike the one that Queenie would give her when displeased with whatever Gidget was doing or attempting to do. But there right in front of her was a very large dog with slick brown hair, large paws, and a curled lip with very large white teeth.

Fortunately, a chain was attached to the collar around its neck as Gidget knew it could make a charge straight at her. She froze in place for a second then backed away slowly maintaining a sharp eye on the dog, wondering what its next move might be. Managing her retreat to not do anything that would provoke the dog, even though it was chained and probably could not reach her, she preferred no confrontational drama and, when safe, turned and made her way back to the doghouse. Though her search was only for a short time, it again produced nothing. She would have to continue to fight the feeling that Queenie was truly gone; she was losing hope and right now felt that her searching was in vain, and Queenie would more than likely never return.

XXX

The soft grass under the small bush in the ditch next to the roadway was warm and soft. It was hard for Queenie to shake off sleep and think about starting out, but there was some kind of a racket in the field next to where she had been sleeping, and it would be impossible to continue resting; but rather than starting out, she sat to observe and find out what the clicking, clacking, and rattling was all about.

There in the field was a tractor with some kind of cutting tool attached, causing the tall mountain hay to fall in a thick straight row after the tractor had made its way through. The sweet smell of the newly cut hay permeated the air. Queenie sat watching for a time mesmerized by the activity. There was no reason to crawl back to her nest and rest because all the noise would make it impossible to get any rest, so it was time to get started. Right now, there was no traffic on the road. She made her way up the bank, onto the pavement, stopping for a short time to tend to the paw that had been punctured by the stubble. For some reason, it was beginning to swell and hurt.

There was something about the day that was different. The fields were filled with what looked like loaves of freshly baked bread assembled from the grass hay harvested from the field. The days were not as hot, and travel during the day now was noticeably more comfortable. Whatever the difference now, it did not mean much. Her stamina seemed to be slowly evaporating, and she could no longer continuously trot down the roadway as she did traveling at night, not taking much time to rest. She hadn't really gone that far having to lay on the edge of the road just for a short rest.

Her ears began to pick up an odd sound coming from farther down the road, so rather than resting, she made an effort to continue on and find out what all the commotion was about. Spotting the source of all the racket, she knew instantly what it was all about and was thrilled to see the gathering of magpies and blackbirds. Her badger dog instincts were beginning to take charge, her energy rebounding as she slowly made her way closer to the prize. Charging toward the birds, lip curled, snarling, and barking, the birds fled to the nearby fence, leaving the meal for Queenie to enjoy. All the birds left except for one.

This bird stood its ground, exhibiting no fear of Queenie even as she backed away preparing for another charge. The bird was much larger than the magpies and blackbirds and exhibited dense black shiny feathers, long black legs, a very strong black beak, and intense black eyes which stared unwaveringly at Queenie. The charge with curled lip and barred teeth came as the bird must have anticipated, spreading its wings and flying just above Queenie, then settling down on the meal signaling to Queenie that it wasn't about to fly off and let Queenie have her way.

Again and again, Queenie charged the bird but to no avail. The bird simply spread its wings and flew high enough to avoid the assault. Queenie was tiring, but the badger dog simply was not about to back down. The bird's steel, cold black eyes gave no hint of backing down either. Queenie circled the meal looking for an entrance and again charged. This time, the bird flew right above Queenie and then, without provocation, pecked her hard on the top of her head, breaking the skin. Queenie fell back, puzzled, trying to regain her composure. She lay shaking her head, trying to determine her next move then noticed that the bird had stationed itself at the far end of the meal. Exhibiting no aggression, Queenie walked up to the side of the meal away from the bird and began devouring what she had not had for some time, a solid, sumptuous meal. When she had filled herself, she backed away, exhibiting no aggression but never taking her eyes off the bird, and the bird did not take its black piercing eyes off of her.

As she made her way down the bank off of the road, the bird called the blackbirds and magpies back. Queenie felt vindicated even if the shiny-feathered big blackbird had impugned her badger dog dignity. She had had more to eat this day than she could remember. How good it felt to have her hunger satisfied. A feeling of euphoria was sweeping over her. Now for a short rest and then to continue on.

Traveling during the day had its advantages. This day was warmer than it had been, and the scenery helped keep her focused on what hopefully would become her final destination. The evening and night skies generally were beautiful, filled with magnificent colors at dusk, watching the moon make its transition from little to no light to a glorious golden glowing lamp and, of course, lots of stars; but being able to see exactly where she was going had great benefits. The season definitely was changing, the paved road not nearly as hot as it had been during the day, and the traffic had diminished. After having had such a wonderful meal and a good rest, she was rejuvenated.

XXXI

She had made her way down the roadway with little to no distraction, but it was becoming more difficult with each step to firmly set her foot solidly on the ground. Her paw was becoming more swollen and hurtful, and this circumstance was disheartening. Regardless, she otherwise felt strengthened and was determined to continue on.

Not too far down the road on the other side of the barbed-wire fence, there was considerable activity involving people. Up to this time, she had not seen or had any encounter with one person since leaving the settlement. Stopping for a short time and observing would give her paw an opportunity to rest. Queenie found a comfortable spot under the barbed-wire fence on the bank of the irrigation ditch. All the activity must involve the mountain hay that had been harvested in the field as tractors were raking the rows of hay lying on the ground into large accumulations that were being gathered at breakneck speed into very large bunches by an odd-looking machine with long wooden tongs on the front, then speeding the large bunch down the field, still at breakneck speed, placing it in front of a huge slide made from long straight poles placed side by side, taking on the appearance of a very big slide then the machine backed away, heading across the field to gather another billowy row.

The hay lay in front of the slide for a very short time when a truck, pushing a long pole with a large bumper on the front, raced its engine then drove at breakneck speed and hit the billowy pile, pushing the hay up the slide that then fell over onto a well-prepared bed. Two men with some kind of tool then spread the hay out evenly. The truck then backed away, waiting for another load of hay. All the activity was quite entertaining to Queenie as she lay on the bank licking her swollen paw, hoping that the swelling would recede, and the pain would go away.

It wasn't long, and she began to ease into a slumber as the activity continued. It did not last long as a stillness began to overtake the field. The equipment was leaving, making its way into another field, leaving the truck to pull the slide away from the stacked hay. When all was loose, there appeared a perfect loaf of newly harvested mountain hay taking on the appearance of a freshly baked loaf of bread storing the winter feed for the cattle that would soon be coming from the mountain pastures. The slide was then attached to the truck which followed the retreating equipment. Only one small truck remained which two young men were about to enter when for some reason they began running in Queenie's direction, shouting, laughing, hollering at the top of their lungs. Queenie was puzzled then realized they were coming for her.

She could hear them calling, "Here, doggy, doggy. Here, doggy, doggy," as one of them stabbed the ground with the tool having long metal tongs attached.

Right then, there was no aggressive badger dog instinct; instead, a wave of fear rushed over her like a raging river. She quickly moved from the ditch bank back under the barbed-wire fence and desperately ran up the short embankment to the road. The euphoria she had felt from her last meal vanished. The infected paw was throbbing like a beating drum. She whimpered with the pain but ran as fast as her miniature dachshund legs would take her down the road-way then dashed to the opposite side of the road, racing down the small embankment into heavy grass where she felt she could hide. She lay close to a fence post in the grass hopeful that she would not be spotted should someone come looking. She lay trembling, panting for air, trying hard to calm herself down. It took time, but as the sun began to fade behind the mountains, Queenie was gaining control, hoping that tomorrow would be a better day.

XXXII

The night had been fitful as her paw had swollen to the size of a burdock blossom, and the throbbing would simply not stop no matter how much she licked it. She lay close to the fence post, trying to decide what to do. A good drink of water wouldn't hurt anything. She made it up onto three paws and was sure she could make it through the pasture when she noticed she was not alone. Not far away were other animals, two of which she was sure had spotted her. She quickly lay down waiting to see what they were going to do when the two calves walked right up to her, sniffing with their large, wet pink noses, then let out a snort and ran away, tails straight in the air.

She was sure they were not going to be a worry when four or five of them came running toward her, stopping short of running over her. Again, their wet pink noses were close but did not touch her. She lay very still, waiting when they all snorted, tails straight in the air, running to the opposite end of the pasture. She was in no condition to move quickly, but it was evident she needed to find cover someplace else.

She continued to make her way across the pasture, trying to maintain some surveillance of where the calves might be, then happening upon a water tank. Circling around the tank, she looked desperately for a place to drink, but there simply was not one. Trying hard to stand just on her hind legs and find a way up to the top of the tank, it was just too tall. With a long sigh, she continued on three legs through the pasture, searching for a secure place to rest.

Her ears perked up as there were dogs barking not too far in the distance. As she limped on, there at the edge of the pasture was a road, and across the road was a ranch house and two dogs waiting impatiently on the porch. It wasn't long, and a man stepped out of the house and called the dogs, which then jumped into the back of the pickup, and all proceeded down the road. Queenie breathed a sigh of relief, making her way out of the pasture. There was a large area around and behind the house that might allow her to find a place where she would not be detected.

Making her way out of sight and quite a distance from the house, she was delighted to find a shed, and next to the shed was a small pond. Trying hard to rush, she could hardly get to the water quickly enough. At the edge of the pond, she pushed her way into the water and there drank her fill. While there, the cool water eased the pain and throbbing in her paw, causing her to remain right where she was. Finally, she decided to withdraw from the water and find a soft place to rest. Limping into the shed, she perused the area then decided to establish her nest in a grassy corner close to the entrance where she was, circled the small area pressing the grass down, then laying down, attending to her paw, then was soon fast asleep.

In what seemed just a very short time, Queenie was startled awake. There in front of her was a gray-and-white face with two short but sharp little ears, two soft sky blue eyes, and a pink nose bordered by a gathering of very long white whiskers on either side. For a short time, the two of them stared intently at each other, then the cat turned and made its way to the opposite end of the shed. For whatever reason, Queenie made no attempt to bar her teeth, curl her lip, or exhibit any badger dog aggression. She merely lay there and observed the cat's destination.

It wasn't long, and she could hear little kitten noises as the mother cat called them in. It must have been feeding time as eventually everything became very quiet. Queenie felt secure because right now she was in a bad way. It was quiet, her nest was warm and soft, and she was soon back to sleep.

XXXIII

The morning sun was shining through the openings between the exterior walls and doorways beginning to warm the interior of the shed.

This was a good place to be. The paw was beginning to respond to soaking in the cool water of the pond when a drink was to be had; there had been an occasional meal and night sounds, which were something that always soothed her. But best of all was the company of the cats. The kittens never came really close, but their curiosity always brought them into view, letting Queenie know what their opinion was with their breathy hisses. The three were little balls of long white fur and soft sky blue eyes just like their mother's.

Each morning, the mother cat would come with a meal and call the kittens into the nest for something to eat. Afterward, she would groom them in preparation for the day. Then she would be gone again, hunting for the next meal, the life of a feral cat. It was hard; she only had herself to depend on to find enough food to maintain herself and her family, but that was how it was. Each day was the same; sometimes there was plenty and often not enough, but they managed.

When the mother cat would leave, the kittens would play, romping with one another, pouncing on a moving piece of grass, any and all antics, thoroughly entertaining Queenie as she lay tending to her paw. The one thing that was quite noticeable was the brown scabby material around the kittens' eyes. They, however, were not concerned about it at all, and it definitely did not interfere with their play.

Soon, all of the activity would quiet the kittens, and it would be no time at all, and they would be napping together in what appeared to be just a big ball of white fur. Watching the kittens was such a pleasure.

Each day was the same routine, going for a drink at the pond, laying on the bank, then slowly moving into the cool water letting the paw soak. The swelling had gone down, and the throbbing and heat in the paw had diminished. After accomplishing the therapy, Queenie would return to her bed, tend to the paw, then have a good nap. She was rejuvenating. Watching the kittens lifted her spirits, and she was beginning to acquire a warm feeling for them. At some time, she would have to leave, but this was the time to enjoy their activity.

There was no change from one day to the next other than it was becoming apparent that fall was definitely in the air. The wind blew more in the afternoon, and the night sounds were not as prevalent. There was one thing that was definitely changing though, and that was the activity of the kittens. They had slowed down considerably, and all three were seldom together as they had been. Perhaps the mother cat was taking one with her to help hunt for a meal.

The day had come, and Queenie was taking a drink at the pond, and her paw would soak for the last time. She lifted herself from the water and made her way back into the shed. Licking her paw, she looked for the kittens, knowing it was the last time she would see them. She remained in her nest wondering why not one made its appearance. It was time to go, and she was standing on all fours, the first time this had happened in a while.

She started walking to the opposite end of the shed where the mother cat had been, but she was nowhere to be seen. There, lying in the grass, were three little balls of fur. Queenie slowly walked toward the kittens, her nose close to the ground, thinking they had already played and were now napping as had always been their routine. She nudged the one, but there was no response. She could see instantly that the kitten's eyes were closed tight by the brown scabby infection, not allowing the kitten to be able to see. She nudged the other two, the situation being the same. Laying down close to the kittens, Queenie was conflicted. She had to be on her way but at the same time did not want to leave these little balls of white fur that had had soft sky blue eyes that she had acquired a warm feeling for. It was quite obvious to Queenie that neither she nor the mother cat would see the kittens ever play again. As grievous as it was, she decided it was time to go.

She turned and left the shed through the door close to the pond, stopping for a last look at the pond and having another good long drink. It had been good to have a nice drink of cool water at any time during the day, to soak her injured paw, to listen in the evenings to the night sounds of the crickets, the frogs, and on occasion the singing of the night bird. She made a wide circle around the shed heading for the road that led to the highway. She definitely did not want to encounter the ranch house should the two dogs be there, and right now, she was in no mood to stir the playfulness of the calves in the pasture.

The day was fading away as she found her way to the highway and started her travel again. The pastures and harvested hayfields were now behind her, and stretched out before her was a long straight roadway and nothing but tall, bushy, sagebrush on either side. It was an almost complete change of scenery from what she had become accustomed to. She knew her paw was not completely healed, but right now, it was holding up, and at least she could travel on all fours.

There was some traffic, but most was on the opposite side of the road, allowing her to remain on the roadway. She was feeling lethargic, burdened, even though she had had a good rest; the pain and burning were gone from her paw, and she was on her way again to find the doghouse and Gidget.

The wind was beginning to pick up and not helping at all. Struggling, she decided to find some type of shelter off the road and rest even if she hadn't gone that far. Maybe the wind would die down, and she would be on her way again. It was easy to lie down under sagebrush off of the roadway and nap which is just what she did. When finally waking up, the wind had died down some, and the sun was filling the sky with red, yellow, and golden clouds before slipping behind the mountains. There was a sound, one she had not heard for a long time. Her ears perked up, wanting to determine that what she was hearing was in fact the coyotes singing. She was stirred then rose from her bed, pointing her nose into the air, and began singing with them. It was a song of melancholy, *yip, yip, awyoo, awyoo, yip, yip, awyoo, awyoo.*

The song was singing away her sadness for Puppy, for Gidget and the doghouse, and for the little balls of white fur with the soft sky blue eyes. The coyotes sang, and she sang with them for a long while then it was time for them to hunt or find their dens, and it was time for her to start her journey again.

XXXIV

Gidget lay at the door of the doghouse, her head on her paws, watching the schoolyard. School had started, and the children were outside playing. Before, she had always made trips by herself to the school grounds to engage with the children who would talk nicely to her, pet her, and sometimes offer her something to eat. She had not gone this fall at all but was beginning to be enticed. The last time she left the doghouse was the last time she had looked for Queenie, to no avail. She was feeling timid about venturing to the schoolyard and perhaps would not go today. But then again, she was very lonely, and having some attention from the children would be such a joy.

She made her way out of the yard and then across the street to the edge of the playground. There was no notice of her by the children until she was almost in the center of where they were playing. Almost everyone stopped what they were doing and stared at this poor little dog, its hair dull and ragged, its ribs and backbone somewhat protruding from under its skin. She was no longer the slick-haired, cute miniature dachshund that had visited the playground before. Suddenly, the children started laughing and pointing at Gidget, some throwing rocks and some kicking dirt in her direction. Thankfully, the children were called, and they raced from the playground back into the school. She sat still wondering why they had not treated her kindly as they always had before. Slowly, she made her way back to the doghouse, crawled onto the green shag rug, and remained there for the remainder of the day. If Queenie had been there, maybe things would have been different.

XXXV

The wind had been blowing every day since she had started down this stretch of road, stirring the dirt and whatever was on or near the road. The surroundings were much different from what she had been used to, nothing inspiring, no smell of sweet clover or freshly mowed mountain hay, or even the smell of sagebrush blooming as that was all that lay in front of her. Generally, when singing with the coyotes, her spirits would be raised, but not this time. Feelings of sorrow and doubt were gripping her and simply would not let go. Right now, she doubted that she would ever find Gidget and the doghouse. But she had to continue on; it was too late to turn back, and she could not remain where she was. The pads on her paws were raw and had been for some time, but she had managed to deal with the soreness; however, the injured paw was beginning to throb again, and that could develop into a real problem.

She continued on the roadway, not at a trot but walking as best she could. She passed two houses on the opposite side of the road, but she had seen ranch houses along her travels before. The wind had finally died down to a gentle breeze, and she was needing to rest. She walked slowly and carefully down the embankment and located a patch of grass, immediately circled the clump to make a nest, and began to lick the pads on her paws. Lifting her nose into the air, she caught the smell of a wonderful aroma. She hesitated then lifted her nose again. What a wonderful smell, the aroma of roast beef. Her wanting for something to eat was beginning to churn. It had been so long since she had had something good and enough to eat. She kept smelling the air, trying to maintain that wonderful aroma. Feeling that she recognized the smell enticed her to abandon the thought of rest and continue on.

Queenie labored to make her way back up the embankment. Much to her surprise, there were several houses scattered out along the opposite side of the highway. Nevertheless, she was more interested in locating where the smell of food was coming from. She was at the edge of the roadway only momentarily observing her surroundings when she heard laughing, shouting, and something being thrown through the air; and a pickup truck was bearing down on her at a high speed. There was no choice but to get back down the embankment as quickly as possible and find somewhere to hide. The pickup raced passed where she had been. Suddenly, there was the screeching of tires, the engine racing, and the pickup backing up, following Queenie as she tried to find some cover.

Bottles were coming her way, being thrown from the pickup, then suddenly there was a blast, striking her in the lower back, ripping through the skin. The force knocked her down, rolling her over. She lay there trying to muster some "badger dog" swagger, but the shock and pain of what had just happened did not allow her. She just lay there, trying to overcome the darkness that was beginning to surround her. The shouting and laughing continued, the pickup engine raced, and again, there was a squealing of tires as the pickup raced off. Eventually, the noise faded into the distance.

Queenie lay very still, trying hard to remain lucid. She began to cry out in pain then lay still, panting hard to shake loose from what had just happened. Overwhelming tiredness took hold, and she made no effort to move. The sun was beginning to go down, and it soon would be dark. This could have been a time to travel, but not this night. This time, she would lay very still, trying not to move, hoping the pain would subside. Even though she was not hidden, she would have to remain through the night right where she was because there was no other choice. The nights were almost cold now. Perhaps by morning, everything would be better.

XXXVI

Gidget lay half in and half out of the doghouse, watching the children at the school playground. Soft Hands was working in the garden, picking the last of the few vegetables still in the ground. Soon, there would be a hard frost, and the garden would be done for another year. Fall was in full bloom; the aspen trees in the yard were beginning to shed some of their leaves; but mainly the trees were filled with the fall colors of red, gold, yellow, and some green.

The water bowl was full, and there was a small amount of food available for Gidget that she hadn't touched and neither had the ants. It was her routine to remain at the doghouse. She had accepted not going to the schoolyard to see the children or to search the neighborhood for Queenie. There was no need because Queenie was gone.

XXXVII

As the sun began to light the morning sky, Queenie's pain had not subsided and, if anything, was worse. There had not been much rest during the night. Her body was shaking as though she were cold, but in fact, there was nothing cold about her. A nice cool drink of water would be wonderful. And she was starving. How many times had she gone this hungry? When was the last time she had had barely enough food to maintain? Her entire life had been about food and eating and eating as much as she possibly could. That time must have been a lifetime ago. Right now, she had to get on her feet, or she would have to remain here in this spot until rescued, and she knew very well that was not going to happen. But she was a badger dog, and a badger dog is relentless, fearless, aggressive, never giving up, never giving in, and never quitting. Somehow, she would make her way.

Her feet were tender, and that paw was ever so hurtful, but she managed to get up and claw her way up the embankment to the highway. As early as it was, there was no traffic. She could then walk on the pavement which helped her situation.

There were more buildings along the road. This must be some kind of settlement and hopefully nothing like the one she left. Again, she encountered that familiar smell, and it was intriguing. If she had the energy, she would find it.

As the day wore on, it seemed she was hardly making any progress. The labor of trotting was out of the question, so walking was about as much energy as she could put out on her miniature dachshund legs, and they did not cover much ground. She no longer made her way up and down the embankment if traffic was coming. It was much easier to just move to the other side of the road. Not much ground had been covered, but she just had to rest. Being on the opposite side wasn't something she was accustomed to, but it was all right. The embankment was not as steep, and the ground was much smoother. If she could find a small patch of grass, it would be time to rest.

Finding a place to lie down, she licked her paws and would like to have done the same to her back, but it was not possible. As she lay there about to doze off, that wonderful aroma of meat cooking moved through the air. Again, she was stirred. Rest would have to wait. Limping over the ground on this side of the roadway was much easier, and she felt much more secure not having to try and claw her way up and down the embankment.

There were one or two more houses that she slowly walked past. The area upcoming seemed familiar, but she wasn't quite sure. The aroma she had been smelling was becoming stronger, and suddenly she knew the doghouse was near.

XXXVIII

Gidget lay in the door of the doghouse as usual with her sad little face, resting on her paws watching Soft Hands working in the yard, cleaning the flowerbeds, and raking the leaves, finishing the fall cleanup. The leaves were raked into a pile and then stuffed into a bag that was then put into the trash can. Gidget made no effort to move out of the way as Soft Hands raked around her and the doghouse.

It had been the same routine now for almost a week. The yard was looking spick-and-span, ready now for winter and snow. Soft Hands was in the shed putting away the yard tools when Gidget dashed from the doghouse, then stood in front poised at full alert, then left the yard at full throttle, racing down the road for almost a block then stopped, barking, crying, whimpering at something in the weeds.

Soft Hands casually followed, puzzled at Gidget's behavior, when she spotted this pitiful bundle of brown hair, a fraction of the size she had been, lying in the weeds as Gidget whined, barked, and cried racing around Queenie, wanting to nudge Queenie, lick her face to let her know how happy she was to see her but kept her distance, knowing that the guttural growl, curled lip, then barred teeth would be coming. Soft Hands' eyes filled with tears, cooing softly, "Queenie, where have you been?" as she reached down to pick up the little dog. Holding her in her arms, Soft Hands gently stroked her and, in a soft, soothing voice, told Queenie that she smelled terrible.

XXXIX

Queenie was gently laid on the grass in the backyard while Soft Hands entered the house for a
large tub and good soap in preparation for a good
bath. Bringing the tub filled with warm water and placing it close to where Queenie was laying, Soft Hands then
placed a bowl of water in front of Queenie for a good drink
then a very small amount of soft dog food which Queenie
devoured in one bite.

Gidget lay quietly watching everything, whining softly,
wanting to let Queenie know that she was in disbelief that
Queenie had come home but feeling a tremendous joy that
she was there but not wanting to make any moves that
would incite Queenie causing her to bar her teeth, curl her
lip, and then the low, guttural growl.

The little dog was placed in the warm bath water, then
gently washed with strong soap and disinfectant just as the
veterinarian had prescribed. The infected paw was examined along with the pads on the rest of her feet, and the
skin on her lower back was gently examined, noting that
nothing but the skin had been damaged, feeling the knot on
her side, and the two wounds on the top of her head which
were slightly infected but healing. She was then placed on

a soft towel and dried. The entire time, Soft Hands shook her head in wonderment at how this little dog had survived whatever ordeals she had experienced. When all was done, Soft Hands leaned close to Queenie and, in a soft, gentle voice, let Queenie know that she smelled so much better.

Queenie then took her place in the doghouse with the soft green shag carpeting for a rest. Gidget timidly moved in next to Queenie but not exceptionally close, knowing the curled lip, barred teeth, and low, guttural growl could come at any time.

XL

Each day, Queenie was healing and becoming stronger as was Gidget. How wonderful to have plenty of food and fresh water to drink. She ate first as was customary but left more than a helping for Gidget, and she neither snapped nor growled at Gidget should she come close. This was puzzling to Gidget, causing her to wonder if this was the real Queenie, *the queen*, or was this some interloper that was lost and just showed up. Time would no doubt tell, but in the meantime, Gidget was ever so happy to have this dog back even if it did not happen to be Queenie.

The pads on Queenie's paws were healing and particularly the infected one as she lay licking each one vigorously. Gidget cautiously came close wanting to help Queenie and lick the damaged skin on her back. She proceeded slowly waiting for the backlash, but it did not come. Ever so carefully, Gidget began to nurse Queenie's back as Queenie lay there nursing her paws. When all was accomplished, Queenie made it to her feet and faced Gidget. Gidget automatically stiffened, knowing what was in store when Queenie began to lick Gidget's face, chest, ears, and neck.

Breathing hard and fear taking hold, Gidget endured the test.

All of this was very puzzling to Gidget, but she remained on guard. Convincing her that there was a change in their relationship was going to take more than the few gestures that Queenie had made.

As both dogs began to fill out, their fall coats becoming thick and shiny, Queenie's shredded lower back skin had healed nicely, and her activity had increased. Queenie was wanting to make the rounds of the neighborhood, seeing Sally and her two little girls, visiting Mrs. Rudy, just being able to smell and perhaps being rewarded with some of her wonderful meat, then visiting the trailer park, checking up on any changes that may have taken place in her absence, and checking on a few other neighbors.

Gidget lay in the doghouse with her head lying on her front paws, watching intently knowing that Queenie had something in mind. As Queenie started out, she gave a *woof, woof* to Gidget, trying to get her attention, wanting her to go along. This was something she had never ever done before. Gidget gave no response and did not move. Queenie came closer and gave the same invitation. Gidget, with some trepidation, got to her feet and followed as Queenie started for the alley. This was totally new to Gidget as she had *never* been invited to go along when Queenie was on an adventure.

Both dogs crossed the alley and made their way toward Sally's, but no one was there, so Mrs. Rudy's was the next destination. Immediately, Mrs. Rudy saw Queenie at the door. She took a small bit of meat, stroked Queenie gently on the head, then spoke to her in a sweet voice, wondering where she had been. She then went back to work. Gidget noticed that she was not noticed, but no matter, she was accustomed to not being invited or noticed. Besides, when they returned to the doghouse, she would get something to eat. It had become customary for Queenie to not empty the dog dish and allow Gidget to have enough to eat her fill.

Each adventure was beginning to go a little farther and last a little longer. Sometimes it would be farther away than the trailer park. Wherever they journeyed, there would be new people who would talk to them in sweet, gentle voices and sometimes, but not always, offering a treat. Today on their way back to the doghouse, they would stop at Mary and Louise's, both living across the street from the doghouse. For Gidget, it was wonderful to be able to go with Queenie because Queenie always knew the best places to go.

XLI

The mornings were becoming frosty, and Soft Hands had prepared the doghouse for the upcoming change. A warm and fluffy dog blanket covered the shag rug in the doghouse, and a door which the dogs could go out of or go in had been installed to keep out the cold fall air.

Each day, both dogs were becoming stronger, much healthier, and more energetic. Their backs were becoming smooth, almost totally covering the protruding backbones, and on the sides, there were no visible ribs. Unbelievably, Gidget's appetite increased, and Queenie's decreased. The dogs were eating together. Something they had never done before, and any adventure Queenie had in mind, Gidget was up for. The first stop would always be Sally's, checking on her and the little girls, and then Mrs. Rudy's. The outdoor oven was now inside for the season, and the wonderful aroma of the cooking meat no longer permeated the outside air, but Mrs. Rudy still enjoyed the visit from Queenie and now Gidget, always offering a treat to both. Then they would go to the trailer park for a visit and treats if anyone offered.

On the return trip from their adventure, Queenie was wanting to play, running and jumping, then circling and barking as she had done with the black-and-white dog. How happy she felt to be home and have Gidget with her. Wanting Gidget to join in, she dashed toward the little dog, jumping up then circling, then running away, and running back trying to entice Gidget to play, but Gidget was having none of it. What was Queenie doing and what was making her act this way? Gathering herself, Gidget made her way back to the doghouse as fast as her short legs would take her. There were just too many changes in Queenie for Gidget to try and comprehend.

XLII

Queenie and Gidget lay under their dog blanket in the doghouse, warm and cozy. Queenie snuggled up close to Gidget, licking her face and ears. It was pleasing to Gidget that Queenie had become so affectionate. Such a change from her previous attitude. Was there going to be an adventure today, and if so, Gidget was wanting to make a trip to the schoolyard when the children were outside playing. Even though her last encounter at the schoolyard had been very disappointing, maybe things would be different now that Queenie was with her.

After a bit of food, Gidget started out on her own toward the school, sure that Queenie would follow. Seeing that Gidget had started, Queenie followed for a while. Suddenly sensing where Gidget was headed and knowing that she and Puppy had been there and had visited some children, she stopped, then barked vigorously at Gidget, wanting her to come back and return to the doghouse. Gidget paid little heed to Queenie's anxiety, thinking she was following close behind. Queenie began to howl, and Gidget stopped. Queenie then moved in close, curled her lip, barred her teeth, and began snapping with a low, guttural growl, letting Gidget know that she had better make it back to the doghouse pronto. Gidget was dumbfounded and devastated by Queenie's behavior. It was a total turn-around from how she had been behaving but maybe she should have expected it all along.

Queenie ran behind Gidget, making sure she did not turn and try to go back to the schoolyard. When Gidget made it to the doghouse, she immediately ran in and hid under the dog blanket. Queenie soon followed and moved in very close to Gidget, licking her face, ears, and chest, nuzzling her, trying to make amends. As pleasant as it was to have the children pay attention to the dogs, pet them, and play, it simply was not a place that the dogs could go. It wasn't long until both dogs were sound asleep, lying very close to each other, succumbing to the stress created by going to the school.

As the day wore on, both dogs, being rested, left the doghouse, Gidget having a good roll in the grass and Queenie itching for another adventure. Queenie started in a direction unfamiliar to Gidget but knowing that Queenie, regardless of her behavior, was still the *queen* and could have her own way once in a while, Queenie barked and whined for Gidget to follow, which she did willingly.

It was almost dusk as they made their way not terribly far from the doghouse to the hill overlooking the river. Queenie sat down at the edge waiting and wanting something special to happen. And suddenly, there it was, the coyotes on the river had begun to sing to one another and to the darkening sky. As Queenie listened, it wasn't long until she pointed her nose straight to the heavens and began to join in the chorus. Gidget listened and looked at

Queenie in amazement. Never before had she heard anything like this and had never observed Queenie participating in such a way, but it was touching and inspiring, and she wanted to join in. The dogs yipped and whoofed right along with the coyotes.

The chorus continued until it was time for the coyotes to make their way back to their dens or to begin the nightly hunt. The singing had put Queenie in good spirits, and she was wanting to play. She was having great fun running, jumping, running in circles, laying down, then crouching and jumping up, barking at Gidget, wanting her to play.

Gidget was inspired and, for whatever reason, joined in. The dogs played all the way back to the doghouse. When they reached their destination, each had a good drink of water and a bite of food, then made their way under the warm dog blanket, lying close to each other, knowing all was well—all was well.

EPILOGUE

Queenie was gone from Memorial Day weekend to the first part of October. The relationship between her and Gidget had changed dramatically, and she never again treated her threateningly or intimidated her. They never again were separated, and if one went, the other accompanied. Neither dog ever had another puppy, nor were they ever seen going to the schoolyard. Eventually, they were taken to Kansas, where they remained—together.

ABOUT THE AUTHOR

Jake Brown was born and raised in the small mountain town in rural Colorado, where the events surrounding Queenie and Gidget unfolded. Jake lived there for the better part of fifty years, was involved in the family business and other business operations which offered stimulating life experiences and opportunities.

Jake now resides in Idaho.